HYMNS

Arranged for Easy Piano by Melody Bober

MW00443164

Now you can play the music from church that you love to hear and sing with the *Pure & Simple* series. Each book features lyrics, suggested fingerings, phrasing, pedal markings, and easy-to-read notation. The solo piano arrangements, which use familiar harmonies and rhythms, will put your favorite melodies at your fingertips quickly and easily.

This volume features beloved hymns, which are an important part of worship services. Hymns are a continuous source of inspiration and have been sung for centuries. Their uplifting lyrics are perfect for personal moments of reflection as well as for sing-along gatherings with loved ones. Additionally, hymns are a staple in any pianist's repertoire of worship songs.

Alfred Music Publishing Co., Inc.
P.O. Box 10003
Van Nuys, CA 91410-0003
alfred.com

Copyright © MMX by Alfred Music Publishing Co., Inc.
All rights reserved. Printed in USA.

No part of this book shall be reproduced, arranged, adapted, recorded, publicly performed, stored in a retrieval system, or transmitted by any means without written permission from the publisher. In order to comply with copyright laws, please apply for such written permission and/or license by contacting the publisher at alfred.com/permissions.

ISBN-10: 0-7390-6710-9
ISBN-13: 978-0-7390-6710-9

CONTENTS

ALL GLORY, LAUD, AND HONOR
with
LEAD ON, O KING ETERNAL

Victoriously

Arranged by Melody Bober

"All Glory, Laud, and Honor"
Music by Melchior Teschner
Words by Theodulph of Orleans

4

lift our bat - tle song. _____

cresc.

Lead on, O King E -

ter - nal, we fol - low not with fears; for

glad - ness breaks like morn - ing wher - e'er Thy face ap -

Be Thou My Vision

Traditional Irish Melody
Arranged by Melody Bober

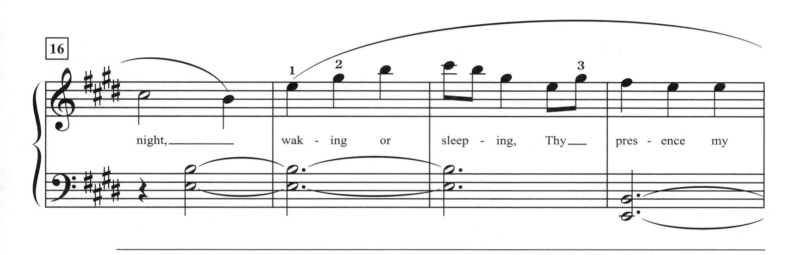

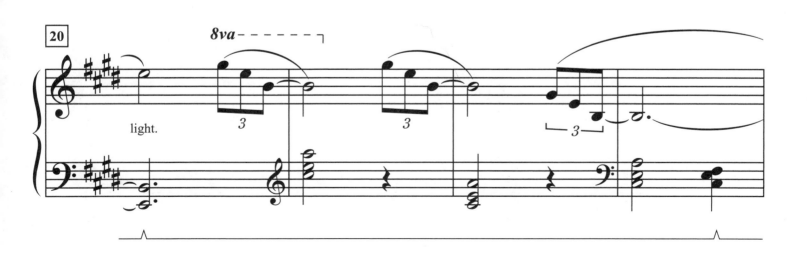

Beneath the Cross of Jesus

Music by Frederick C. Maker
Words by Elizabeth C. Clephane
Arranged by Melody Bober

way   from the   burn - ing   of   the   noon - tide

heat   and the   bur - den   of   the   day.

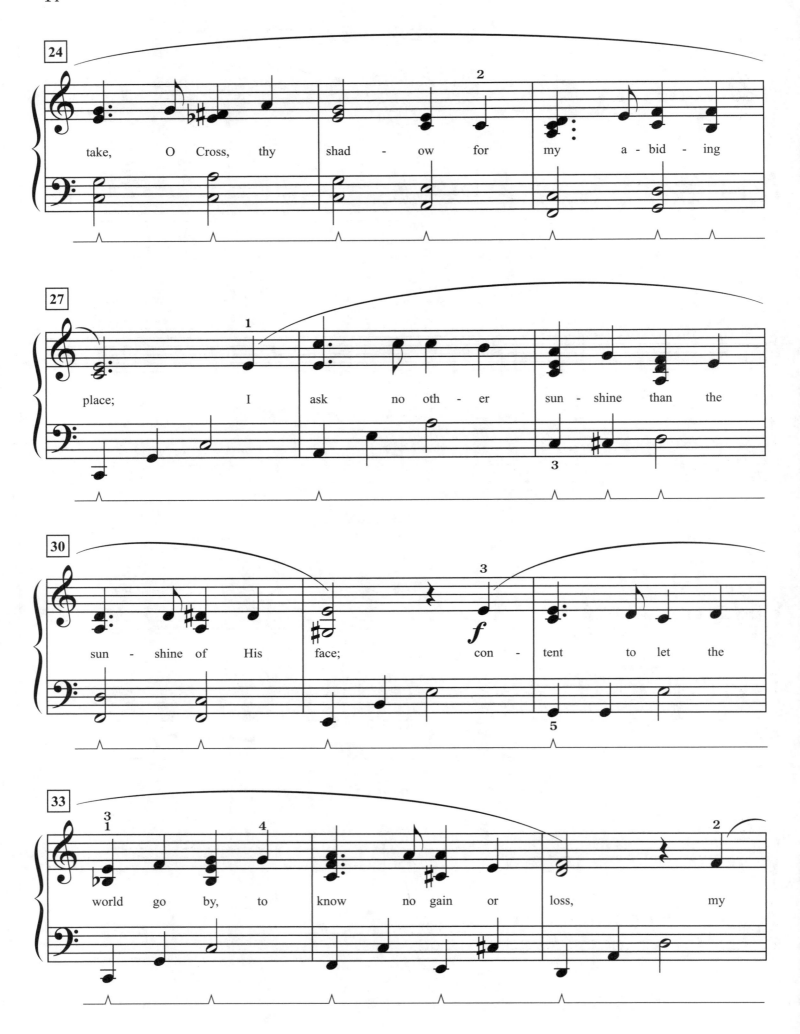

take, O Cross, thy shad - ow for my a - bid - ing

place; I ask no oth - er sun - shine than the

sun - shine of His face; con - tent to let the

world go by, to know no gain or loss, my

sin - ful self my on - ly shame, my

glo - ry all the cross.

poco rit. *mp* *a tempo* *mf* *poco rit.* *p*

COME, CHRISTIANS, JOIN TO SING

Traditional Spanish Melody
Words by Christian H. Bateman
Arranged by Melody Bober

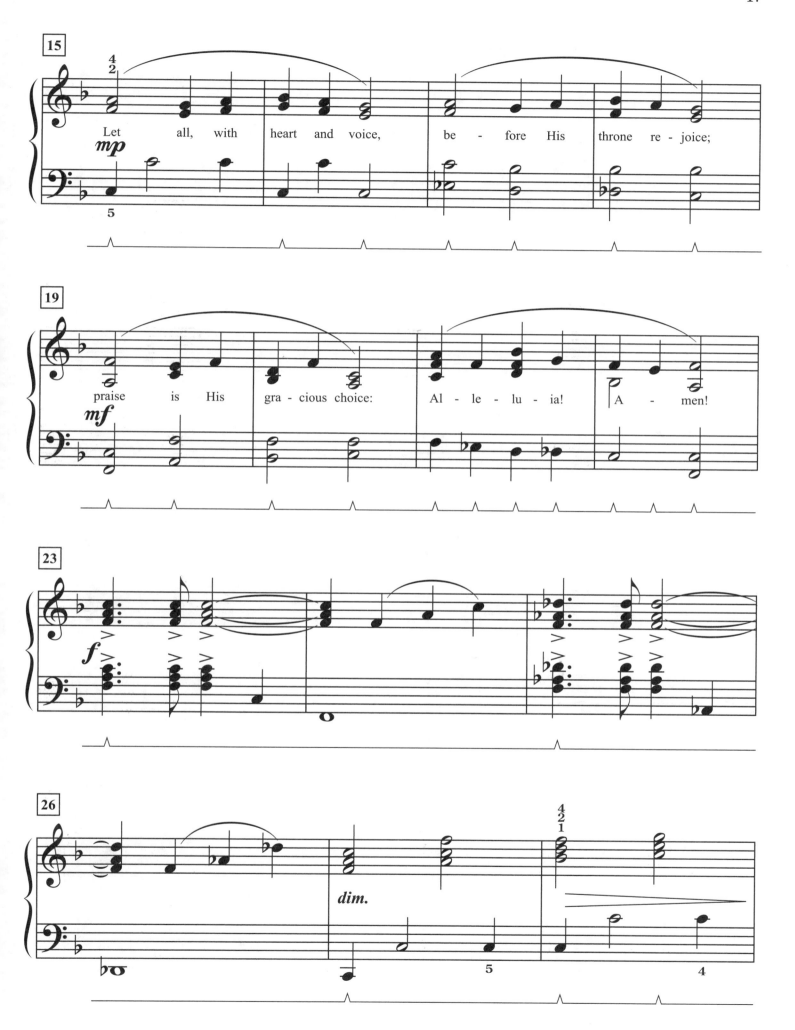

Let all, with heart and voice, be - fore His throne re - joice;

praise is His gra - cious choice: Al - le - lu - ia! A - men!

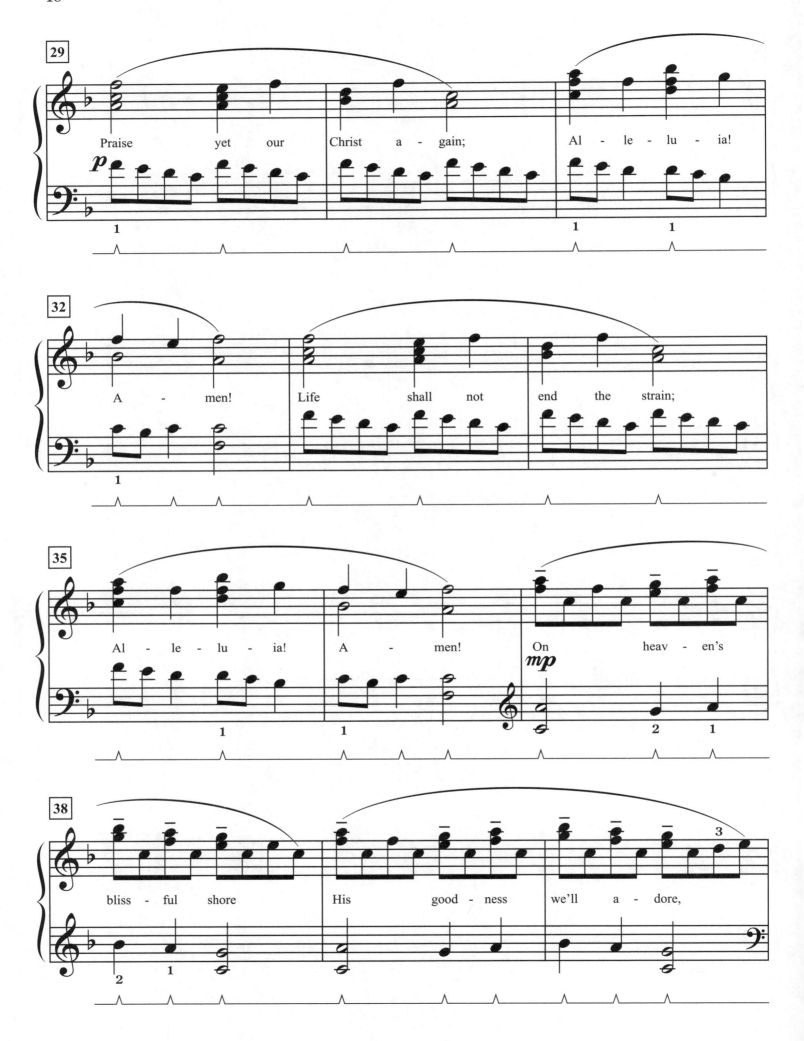

sing - ing for - ev - er - more, "Al - le - lu - ia!

A - men!"

FAIREST LORD JESUS

Music: *Schlesische Volkslieder*
Words: *Münster Gesangbuch*
Arranged by Melody Bober

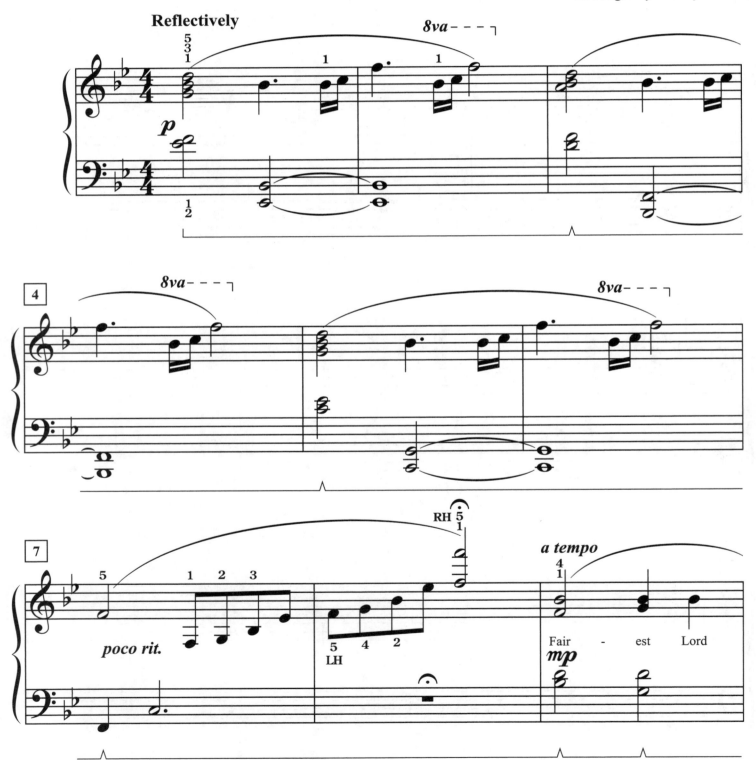

and for - ev - er - more be Thine!

GUIDE ME, O THOU GREAT JEHOVAH

Music by John Hughes
Words by William Williams
Arranged by Melody Bober

Joyful, Joyful, We Adore Thee

Music by Ludwig van Beethoven
Words by Henry Van Dyke
Arranged by Melody Bober

I NEED THEE EVERY HOUR

Music by Robert Lowry
Words by Annie S. Hawks
Arranged by Melody Bober

come ___ to Thee. O bless me now, my
Sav - ior, I come ___ to Thee.

IMMORTAL, INVISIBLE, GOD ONLY WISE

Traditional Welsh Melody
Words by Walter Chalmers Smith
Arranged by Melody Bober

hid from our eyes, most bless - ed, most glo - rious, the

an - cient of days, al - might - y, vic - to - rious, Thy

great name we praise.

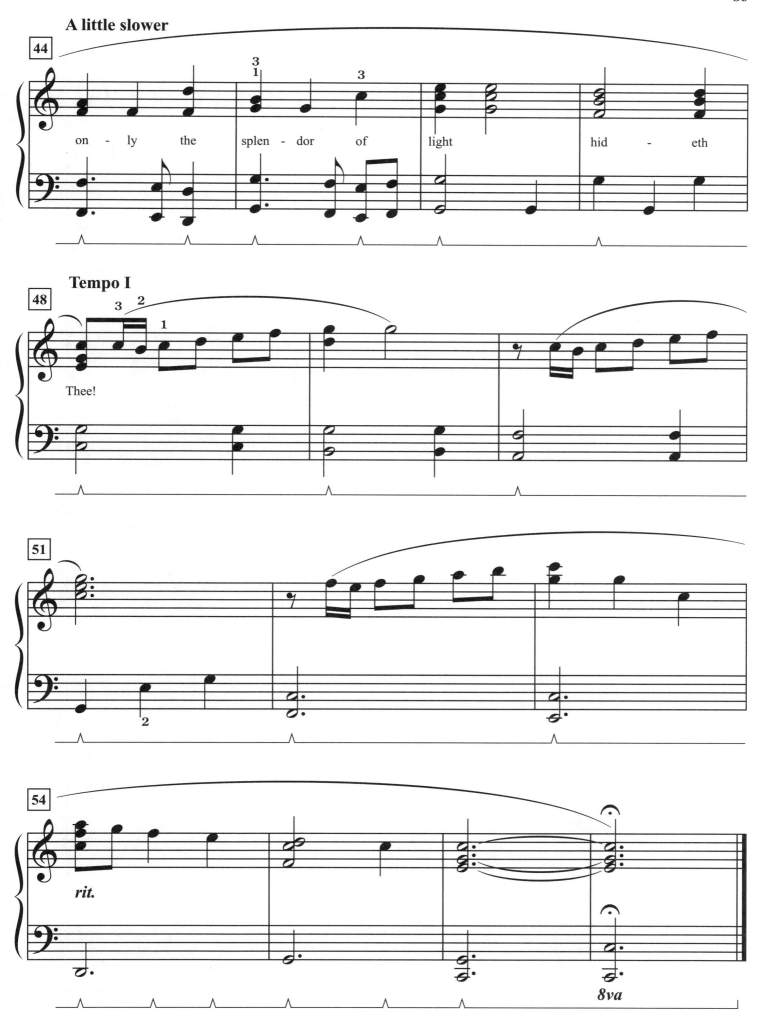

Jesus Is All the World to Me

Words and Music by
Will L. Thompson
Arranged by Melody Bober

glad;   He's   my   friend.

dim.   p

mp

LOVE DIVINE, ALL LOVES EXCELLING

Music by John Zundel
Words by Charles Wesley
Arranged by Melody Bober

Love di - vine, all loves ex - cell - ing, joy of heav'n, to earth come_ down;

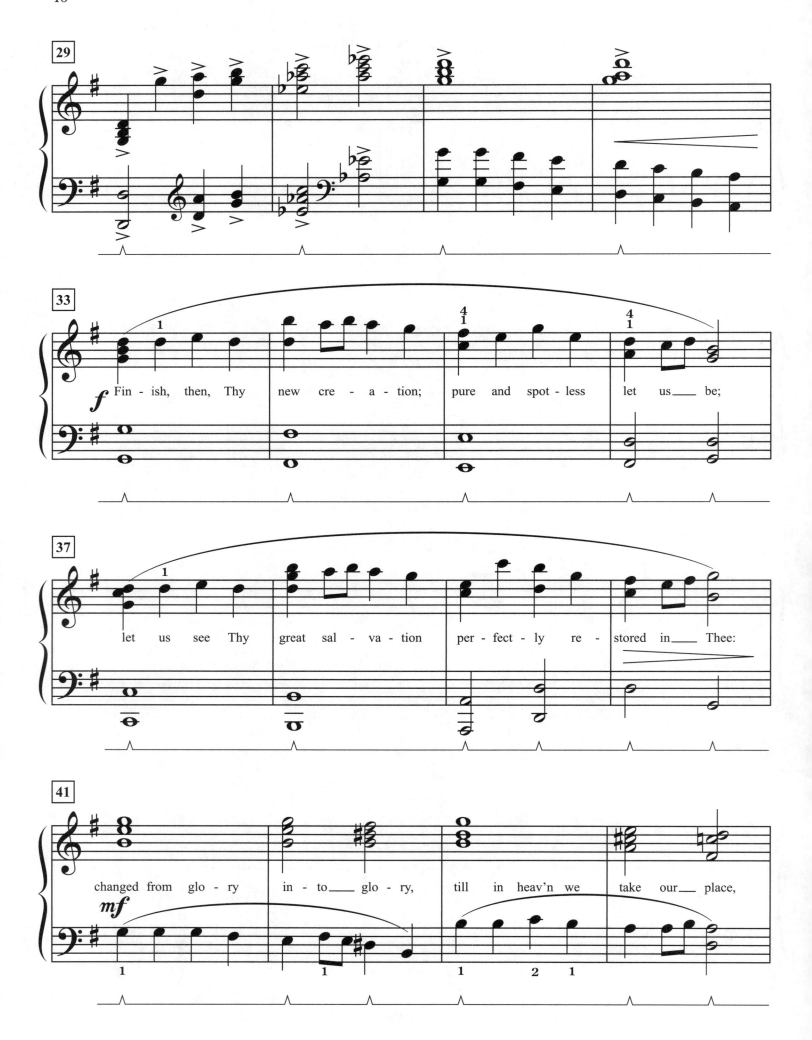

My Faith Has Found a Resting Place

Music by André Grétry
Words by Lidie H. Edmunds
Arranged by Melody Bober

MY SAVIOR'S LOVE

Words and Music by
Charles H. Gabriel
Arranged by Melody Bober

stand a - mazed in the pres - ence of Je - sus the Naz - a -

A New Name in Glory

Words and Music by
C. Austin Miles
Arranged by Melody Bober

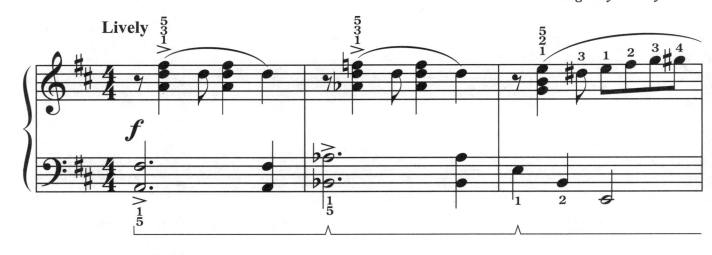

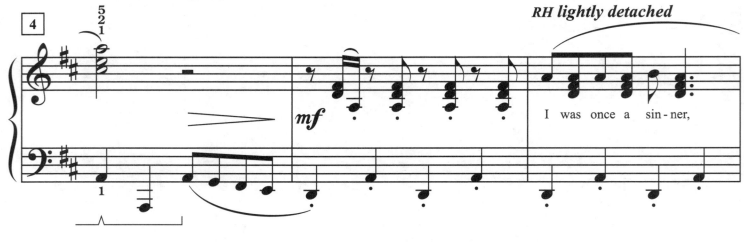

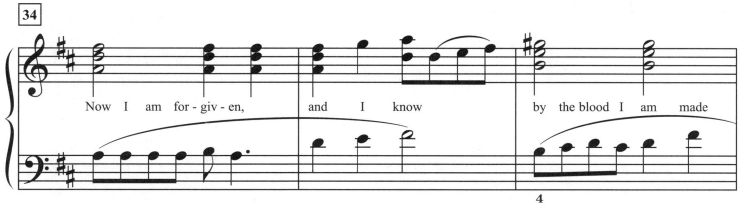

Now I am for-giv-en, and I know by the blood I am made

whole. *cresc.*

D.S. al Coda

There's a

Coda

ff

O THE DEEP, DEEP LOVE OF JESUS

Music by Thomas J. Williams
Words by Samuel Trevor Francis
Arranged by Melody Bober

62

PRAISE HIM! PRAISE HIM!

Music by Chester G. Allen
Words by Fanny J. Crosby
Arranged by Melody Bober

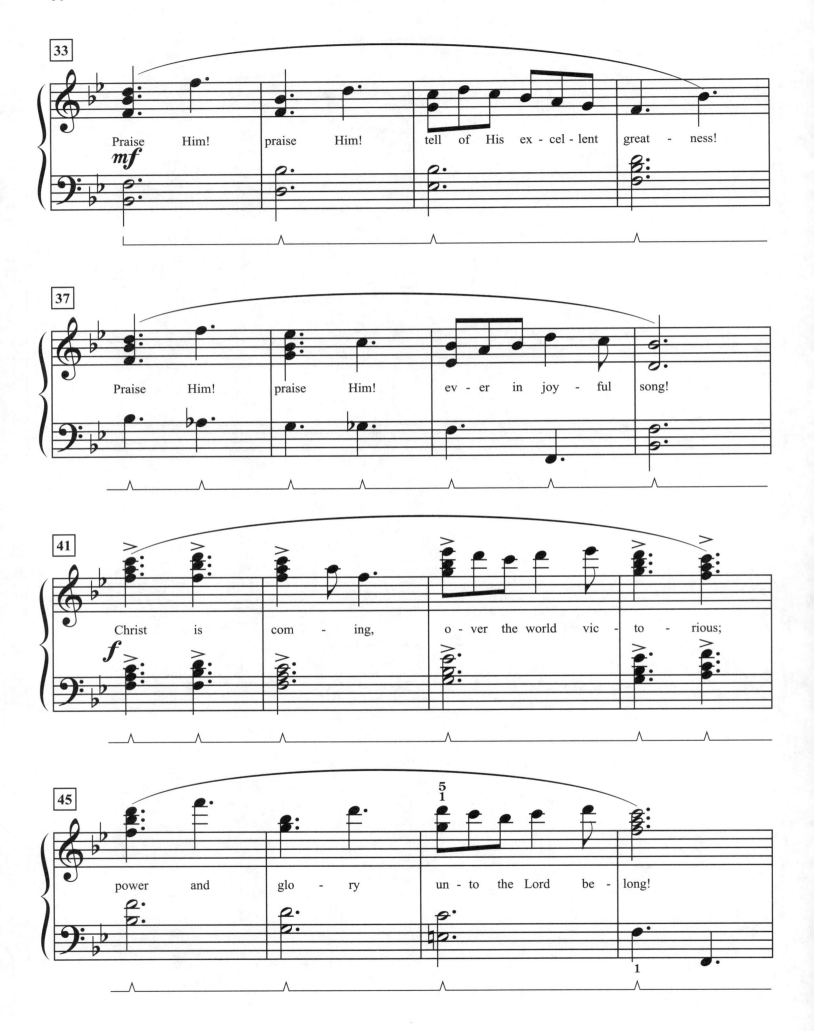

PRAISE TO THE LORD, THE ALMIGHTY

Music: *Stralsund Gesangbuch*
Words by Joachim Neander
Arranged by Melody Bober

70

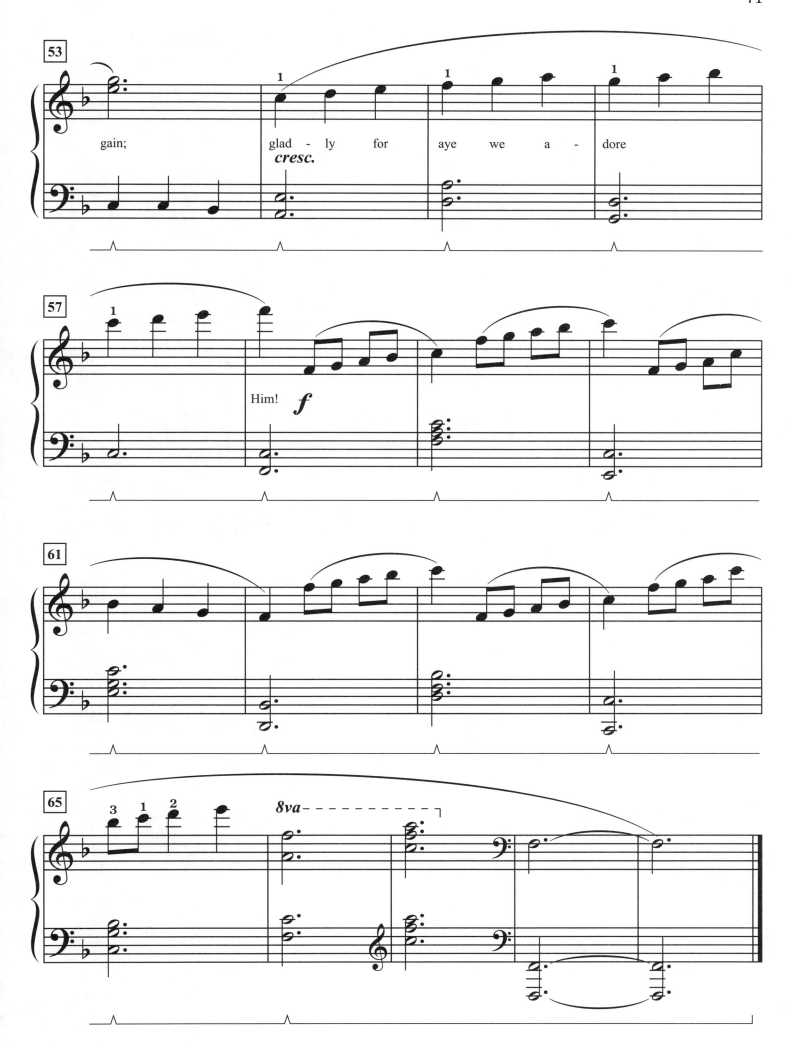

gain; glad - ly for aye we a - dore

cresc.

Him! *f*

THERE IS A FOUNTAIN

Traditional American Melody
Words by William Cowper
Arranged by Melody Bober

To God Be the Glory

Music by William H. Doane
Words by Fanny J. Crosby
Arranged by Melody Bober

78